HEART'S ALCHEMY

HEART'S ALCHEMY

5 *Core Insights* to Seeing Yourself as You Really Are

"Transforming Hearts. Transforming Lives"

DEBORAH S. HOWELL

Published by Victory in Action LLC, Las Vegas, Nevada
© 2014 by Deborah S. Howell
Printed in the United States of America

ISBN: 978-0-9829284-7-9 (paperback)
      978-0-9829284-9-3 (ebook)

Cover and Interior Design by Carolyn Sheltraw
www.csheltraw.com

Victory in Action image created by Michelle K. Ponimoi

Photos of Deborah Howell (back cover) taken by Michael Gordon

VICTORY IN ACTION®

VICTORY IN ACTION® and its image is a registered trademark owned by Deborah Howell

Emotional Muscle Fitness® is a Registered Trademark owned by Deborah S. Howell

Disclaimer: The content in this book is NOT INTENDED as medical advice or to diagnose, treat, cure, or prevent any medical or mental condition. It is NOT in any way intended as a substitute for medical or psychological counseling. The suggestions, ideas, and exercises shared in this book have been helpful to me, but may not have the same benefit for you. You should consult with a licensed physician for anything that relates to your overall health, which includes appropriate medical treatment or any anticipated/planned changes to your diet or exercise routine.

∞ The paper used in this publication meets the minimum requirements of the American National Standard for Information sciences—Permanence of Paper for Printed Library Materials, ANSI Z39.48-1992.

www.victoryinaction.com

DEDICATION

I DEDICATE THIS BOOK TO MY DEAR friend Shirley. Your sudden and unexpected transition jolted my heart and mind wide open to deeply feel and see, to be with life's unpredictability and uncertainty. You gave me a gift of revelation, to recognize the capacity of my heart and engage in the silent presence of pure love and connection. I thank you for your quiet and empowering confirmation of a Divine truth I have known and for being a true friend.

To my family and friends, patients and clients, and to all of YOU who have touched my life and who will be touched by this book, know that you are loved and appreciated! I desire that this book will inspire and encourage you to believe in yourself. May it offer you comfort and companionship, as it offers you insight and enlightenment to a life of love, happiness, peace, and purpose!

Much Love and Gratitude!

ACKNOWLEDGMENTS

I am so blessed and grateful for the love of ALL my family and friends!

Thank you to my husband and to my four magnificent daughters for the daily reminder of what really matters. Whatever challenges we may encounter are all lessons to help us grow and expand our awareness, love, and appreciation. I appreciate your love, support, and patience with me as I explore new insights and opportunities that open to me—to further seek, understand, and express that which desires expression through me, through my voice…

Love and gratitude for my mother. I sincerely thank you, Mom, for taking time to help me edit this book. I am very grateful for your attention to detail and more personally, your love and genuine interest in my pursuits.

Sincere gratitude for my graphic designer, you have helped me to bring my insights to life. Your natural talent and patience have been greatly appreciated!

TABLE OF CONTENTS

MIRROR OF TRUTH — Reflections of the Heart

"Transforming Hearts.
Transforming Lives"

PREFACE
SEE YOURSELF IN THE
LIGHT OF YOUR TRUTH

PEACEFUL REVELATION:

I have listened closely to hear you speak about your challenges and struggles. I share with you a personally meaningful 'aha' experience which I feel may offer you insight... I have been in the process of releasing expectations and familiar patterns and beliefs, to open myself deeply to discover that less is more, simplicity is profound, and ease instead of effort is an experience available to me and available to all who choose to BE present with this knowledge. My background is in physical therapy and I work in an inpatient rehabilitation facility with people virtually starting over from major life-altering situations. Although my knowledge of the body, cellular memory and the nervous system is extensive, it has not been enough. My personal familiarity with feeling ready to move on yet stuck in the long-term physical, mental and emotional struggle has been a significant challenge for me for over a decade. It has been quite the journey. We reach a point of feeling that we are sick and tired of feeling sick and tired; exhausted, in pain and feeling discouraged! We have to recognize that our *pain* and *struggle* serves us until we are truly ready to release it -- it protects us, validates us, reminds us... however, what we know to do for relief is to push it away, ignore it, suppress it, or numb it, not realizing that we can communicate with it. We can come into a dialogue of gratitude and appreciation and validate "its" efforts on our behalf. Let us learn to openly observe and be grateful for this beautiful, loving process. There is a familiarity your body knows and a belief that your mind holds. Trust is at the heart and in the heart of this union you are to make; to release what no longer serves you at your Highest... It is in the Being, the meeting and aligning of your mind with your body (your whole Self) to journey together to allow you to discover a path of ease versus the familiar path of struggle. Intend on a peaceful union with open, honest communion—"Integration." We tend to expect that the journey out of our struggle takes great effort and possibly more struggle because of the length of time or the depth of our pain, for this known way is familiar. Be kind and compassionate with yourself. Simply consider there is another way. May you discover the gentle flow, the light, the presence of love, ease and peace that is you BEING the JOY you are, my friend! We journey together.

"Most of the shadows of this life are caused
by our standing in our own sunshine."

~Ralph Waldo Emerson

I
PERSPECTIVE MATTERS

BE WHERE YOU ARE

Trust that where you are at this moment in your life is where you are to be. Be still and fully present with yourself . . . all that is you, no judgment. Allow for the light of a new day to enter in and warm your heart, drawing in peace and tranquility with each full breath you take. Recognize that through your greatest challenges and adversities, through the darkest of nights, peeks the dawn of a new day. Know that which you long for is already there, patiently waiting for your acknowledgment. You may be looking outward for it, but it resides within you. You have to develop a deeper awareness in order to tap into it, connect with it, and to embrace it, whatever "it" is.

The depths of despair and devastation can be ripping and gouging beyond measure, impairing or paralyzing your thoughts and actions, leaving you with a learned sense of helplessness and hopelessness, believing a myriad of altered "false" truths. Therefore, it is essential you learn how to lovingly and respectfully delve deeper into your soul, your "being" beyond the flesh.

Allow for the entrance into a visceral depth, a "gut" depth, a level that allows you to fully engage and be present with your authentic self, your personal truth. You have the ability to break through undesired patterns of behavior, reorganize, and reestablish new neuronal patterns affecting your body's interpretation. An example of an undesired pattern of behavior is seen when someone has an involuntary "pull away" reaction to touch, where touch is felt as being painful, uncomfortable, or noxious. With this hyper-reactive conditioning, retraining the nervous system through specific desensitization techniques can facilitate a more neutral or normal response, where the same touch stimulus is now felt as being pleasant and comfortable. Hyper-reactive conditioning such as this can be brought about through traumatic experiences that are harsh, aggressive, shocking, violent, frightening, or repetitive in nature. It can also result from a head injury, spinal cord injury, or direct nerve injury. You can sometimes find yourself with another type of undesirable behavior or state, due to a built-in protective response, intended for your own good initially. This protective state, if left "on," leaves you in a heightened autonomic state, referring to the sympathetic nervous system, where feelings of overwhelm, uncertainty, anxiousness, or restlessness may become your new baseline for coping with life's challenges.

TRUSTING THE PROCESS

Be Mindful of Your Emotions . . . Be at Ease Within . . . Breathe Easy.

There is breadth and depth to our individual and collective lives, which may seem beyond our immediate understanding. Our awareness and capacity will expand as we begin to pay closer attention, learn how to be quiet, engage, listen, and feel with our heart—with our being—being fully present wherever we are.

So often, we live our lives feeling insecure, uncertain, jealous, and resentful. We may frequently doubt ourselves, our friends, or our loved ones. Learning to trust starts with the trust we have with our *self*. Trust and acceptance go hand in hand. We are born with the desire and capacity to love and be loved. Our being or "beingness" thrives on love, for love nurtures, energizes, nourishes, and heals. Trust and acceptance naturally sprout from our ability to connect to, and acknowledge love. Insecurity, supported by a poor sense of self and self-worth, lends to struggles with self-esteem and self-image. Feeling jealous, becoming easily offended, reacting with a quick temper, or never feeling satisfied are some of the emotions and behaviors we often see as a result. It is imperative we take the time to be still, to look inward and tune in to a deeper personal awareness; otherwise, we will continue to look outside of ourselves to find answers, to find our worth, to find blame, to criticize, to oppose, to resent, to judge, and to condemn.

Over the years, I have developed an intrigue as well as an affinity for water. I have found water to be relieving and calming when I drink it, bathe, or shower in it. When at the beach or out on the ocean, I find it calming and awe-inspiring to look at the water. I have discovered a wonderful parallel to our lives, considering the human body is mostly water. Let us recognize that within the core of our "fluid being" lives a powerful, yet gentle and vulnerable spirit. The simplicity, yet significance of our human experiences can be appreciated through the extraordinary similarities of the ocean body relating to its presence and behavior.

Every day presents an opportunity for personal growth, a new perspective, and, yes, a fresh start. We must allow ourselves to grow and blossom from any experience, however painful or devastating it may be. We eat away at our livelihood and carry a great burden when we harbor destructive emotions for extended periods of time. Before we know it, we find ourselves held hostage to the cold, dark emptiness of a broken and wounded heart, an aching soul, a lifeless spirit. When we avenge or bring others down, we tear down ourselves in the process. We grow bitter and weary as we use up our vital resources from this toxic and negative energy, ultimately depleting ourselves, and stagnating our growth. Look not to judge, condemn, or seek revenge, as these behaviors do not serve our greater good. They serve to destroy the heart and soul, separating us from our joyous spirit, cheating us out of life's opportunities for personal growth, healing, and fulfillment. Seeking forgiveness, finding compassion and empathy in the warmth of its healing energy, begins to release us from the bondage of deeply, painful emotions such as anger, guilt, shame, despair, and resentment. Forgiveness is our prescription for salvation. It is the salve for our soul, the balm with which we soothe our open wounds.

The most valuable gift we can give to each other is trust. Not trust in the sense that we won't make mistakes but trust that the tenderness, fragility, and vulnerability of our deepest heartfelt emotions will be honored and valued as if they were our own. We are interdependent beings all capable of giving and receiving this wonderful gift. True, authentic, and unconditional heart-to-heart connections convey without words *acceptance*, and have an undercurrent of love, compassion, empathy, and appreciation. This way of relating opens the door to trust and forgiveness, to hope and possibility, to a new friendship or intimate relationship. Tears may flow so that hearts may grow.

We can all learn how to trust, allow ourselves to access and embody a true sense and *state* of trust with desired intention and practice. Studies have shown that our life experiences, conditioned behaviors, and emotions have an effect on our biochemistry and physiology. There is actual research on the biochemistry of trust that has examined the hormone-neurochemical, Oxytocin.[1,2] In the article titled, *The Neurobiology of Trust*, Paul J. Zak discussed how Oxytocin could increase both trust and trustworthy behavior.[3]

FIND PEACE AND PURPOSE

Recognize that the lack of fundamental awareness is supported by stagnant and congested thoughts and reinforced by more of the same. When you choose to remain in the dark, this permits for denial, avoidance, and hiding of truths; overshadowing and clouding your vision for what is available to you through divine inheritance. It is important for you to recognize what you do have and what you can be grateful for right now. This is not based on your external conditions. This is about your inner resources and influences that support and inspire you. Many of you know that your external conditions influence how you feel, but it is important for you to recognize and appreciate what you have in this present moment, "what is," the bare essence and presence of your heart and soul, stripped of any external influences. Peace and purpose will show up with your commitment and are supported by appreciation and acceptance as their foundation. This platform provides stability and enables mobility which helps you to rise up and move forward fully and freely.

BE AWARE OF YOUR CONNECTIONS

- *What are you connecting to?*
- *Where are you looking, what are you waiting for, what are you using to gauge a sense of peace and happiness?*
- *Do you place conditions on yourself or others before you can achieve happiness and peace?*

Here are examples of CONDITIONAL Happiness and Peace Statements:

(Fill in the blanks):

"I would feel secure if my _____ gave me more attention."

"I would be satisfied if my _____ would support me."

"I would be less frustrated if my _____ would listen to me."

"If I just had more _____ then I'd be happy."

"If I just had less_____ then I could _____."

"If I just had more _____ then I could _____."

"I would feel better if I had more _____."

"I would be happy if _____."

"My life would be great if _____."

"My life would be better if _____."

The idea of drawing your attention to these CONDITIONAL statements is to have your awareness of simple language that reinforces UNDESIRED outcomes. The type of questions we ask or statements we make affect our outcomes. You can choose to have external conditions add to or take away from your life and livelihood. It is a practice and a process to choose only the things that contribute to your well-being. I have personally made a decision to not let undesirable conditions and circumstances take away from my life, but I will allow them in some way to add to my life. Do your very best to give your very best in all you do. Pay a compliment or offer a kind word to those that hurt you. Never wish ill will against anyone, no matter what! Never give up on yourself! Allow for the presence of inner peace and tranquility to weave throughout the fabric of your being. Peace and happiness are achieved through an inner knowing, an inner wisdom, and sensing purpose and gratitude for what is, submitting to and accepting the now. You must practice going beyond the image, beyond the words, beyond the transgressions, into the heart of the spirit of compassion.

- *What would happen if an accident, a sudden death, or a natural disaster were to enter into your life and take away or drastically change what you know and believe?*
- *What would matter to you at that very moment?*

- *What would you think about at that very moment?*
- *What would become your priority?*

Realize peace and purpose right here and now. You have the opportunity to open up to the light of a new day. Begin to clear space and remove clutter to make room for clarity and insight. Open up so the "light" energy can flow throughout, and take a few slow deep breaths, breathing in gratitude and exhaling appreciation. Seek to learn and practice the art of tuning in. Commit to living with inner peace and serenity.

"Peace in our families, communities, and throughout the world begins with our INNER Peace."

"Should you shield the canyons from the windstorms you would never see the true beauty of their carvings."

~Elisabeth Kubler-Ross

I See You

I Know You

You are Me

Together are We

We are One

ONE Family...

II
FEELINGS and EMOTIONS

WOUNDS OF THE HEART

Most of us have been hurt or have hurt someone in our lifetime. Many of our hurts are from the people closest to us, oftentimes our parents, our spouses, and our children. Some of these hurts have been resolved and amends have been made; however, many of them are unresolved, carried along, harbored, and reenacted in some way. The pain from being hurt stays alive and present, influencing our decisions, feelings, and behaviors. For example, as an adult, now a parent, you may find yourself reliving your childhood through your child. You may be treating your child as you were treated or completely go in the opposite direction of how you were treated, or maybe you are trying to make your child out to be what you wanted to be, or make your child do what you did not get to do, and have the things you wanted to have when you were a child.

- *Do you want your child to do as you did when you were his or her age?*

- *Are you reliving your childhood hurts through your child?*
- *Are you passing on your hurts to your child?*
- *Are you living through your child?*

In intimate relationships:
- *Have you set up barriers because you are expecting to be hurt?*
- *Are your defenses up because of previous hurts?*
- *Are you trying to avoid ever getting hurt again?*
- *Are you minimizing risk of getting hurt?*
- *Do you trust yourself to handle getting hurt again?*
- *Are you open to trusting in any intimate relationship?*
- *Are you avoiding intimate relationships all together?*

Wounds can run deep, so deep they lodge within the core of our being, in our cells, and tissue memory. As a way to cope or compensate, we unconsciously create a thick barrier of protection through pride, ego, and other defense mechanisms to allow us to keep functioning and pressing forward. The reservoir of energy, the "charge" contained in these wounds can be so powerful, somewhat of a volcanic nature or similar to the magnitude and intensity of a tornado or the magnificent swell and roar of the ocean's tidal waves during a storm.

- *How do we begin to open up and release?*
- *How do we let go when the slightest comment, behavior, circumstance, or gesture — anything that triggers painful emotions or hints at poking into our wounds — elicits a defense reaction, a surge of pride, and has us put on our armor to protect and shield us from further anguish, despair?*
- *What are we to do when feelings begin flooding us, feelings that represent a combination of anxiety, animosity, guilt, resentment, disappointment, betrayal, disgust, anger, hurt, frustration, overwhelm, fear, pain, despair, and hopelessness?*

Bitterness, hatred, and resentment are toxic emotions that burn their way into the creation of a self-inflicted wound.

- *How much energy is carried in those feelings you harbor deep within your body?*
- *What would an eruption of this energy feel like, look like, and act like?*
- *Do you feel like you are going to burst?*
- *How much negative emotion can one body contain before physiologically feeling like doing something really drastic and life altering, either to yourself or someone else?*

YOU CAN MEND A BROKEN HEART

A broken heart can be a very physically painful experience. This type of pain is known as heartache. It is a deeply felt ache that grabs hold of your attention and may feel like it is more than you are able to bear. During such a time, soften into your heart and meld with your pain as if you are gently cradling and rocking a baby. Allow your tears to flow and let sounds from your heart release through sobbing, moaning, groaning…offering unconditional tenderness and compassion for yourself during this time. You have to allow yourself time to acknowledge what you feel, to go through the emotions. Emotions can vary in duration and severity. All kinds of feelings can process through a broken heart. You may experience despondency, despair, severe sadness, pain, grief, anger, resentment, or guilt. Be kind, gentle, and patient with yourself so that you can hear your truth, and validate and recognize your worth. Prayer, meditation, or periods of silence can be helpful. Know that you are innately wise beyond your own understanding.

Most of us have had our hearts broken more than once. The uncertainty of life events and experiences can show up suddenly, without warning and whether or not we are prepared. This may leave us feeling blindsided, shocked, or devastated. The reality is that life's uncertainty and unpredictability is as natural and commonplace as skinning our knee or getting a paper cut. You are not alone. Life does go on and you will go on too. Finding your way into a level of appreciation and acceptance will support your healing, and allow you to move through and move forward in your life. It is important to seek out positive resources and influences that will offer you a new perspective on your situation. This could be as simple as stepping outside to experience the sunlight on your face or taking a bath or shower and really feel and appreciate the sensation of the water touching your body. Take some time to spend quietly with yourself.

- *Are you dealing with a broken heart or heartache right now?*
- *Are you pushing away or repressing any emotions that feel painful or evoke upsetting memories?*

Make time to take care of yourself. Become your own best friend. Get out and do things you enjoy. Whether it is a broken heart from a relationship, a betrayal, rejection, disappointment, death, or divorce, whatever the reason for the broken heart, it is imperative you find a way to see your situation for how it may positively serve your life. See yourself mending and healing your heart. A broken heart experiences physical pain. Nonetheless, it is important you do not allow yourself to remain in the same situation for too long. You can develop patterns of behaviors and habits that will reinforce a sense of loss, brokenness and possibly, a sense of failure or a sense of unworthiness. Whatever your sense may be, typically, the unconscious coping tendency is to develop habits, patterns, and behaviors that match to how you feel about yourself and the situation. Instead, see yourself on the mend, see yourself healing, and see yourself restoring your life. Seek to forgive yourself and forgive others. It is only natural when you have been badly hurt, to try and minimize or avoid any risk of feeling those same painful feelings over again. In order to rise above and beyond the pain, you have to see yourself moving through the pain, and physically, you have to get your body moving. Simply stepping outside into the sunshine can offer you a different perspective. Learn to appreciate the lesson or lessons from the experience. It may be subtle or profound, however, each lesson helps to make you wiser, more capable, and more knowledgeable, leading you to a greater understanding of yourself and your self-worth. If you look to seek this sort of understanding, you can lessen your pain and gain from the experience.

"What hurts you blesses you. Darkness is your candle."

~Rumi

"There is no coming to consciousness without pain."

~Carl Jung

REFLECTION OF WHAT HURTS

The following is an open and honest contribution
from an amazing 10-year-old child.
Can you relate to the heartfelt emotions in this list?

What Hurts? Feeling like no one cares about you!
What Hurts? People like your friends talk about you behind your back!
What Hurts? Having your friends tell secrets about you, to nosey
people!
What Hurts? Not making your own choices!
What Hurts? Name Calling at school!
What Hurts? Getting dumped at the dance!
What Hurts? Having your crush move away!
What Hurts? Crying if a friend moves away and never sends you mail!
What Hurts? When mommy and daddy fight!
What Hurts? Thinking about bad thoughts like death!
What Hurts? Feeling like someone smaller than you doesn't listen to
you!
What Hurts? People tell you that you're ugly or you just don't fit in!
What Hurts? Not being answered!
What Hurts? Following trends instead of setting trends!
What Hurts? Knowing that you have lots of problems in your life!
What Hurts? Not having anyone support you!
What Hurts? Not getting your way!
What Hurts? Losing your stuff!
What Hurts? Being afraid to show the real you!

Truly, we are all children in grown-up bodies.
We have the same feelings and emotions as we did
when we were children — the same things matter!

III
FORGIVENESS

THE ESSENTIAL INGREDIENT

Forgiveness is an essential ingredient to personal growth, good health, and healing. We must forgive ourselves and others for wrongdoings and hurtful actions. Harboring hurt, disappointment, anger, and guilt will slowly eat away at the quality of one's life. On a larger scale, we can find generational and cultural issues of forgiveness that have yet to be resolved or put to rest in our hearts.

- *Why is it so difficult to forgive?*

Keep in mind that when you choose to hold fast to judgment of right or wrong, just or unjust, fair or unfair, you close yourself off to healing. Your resistance will slowly deplete your energy, stagnate your inner growth, and keep your joyful spirit from reviving. Recognize why you are choosing this path of pain, and decide to heal and restore your life. Forgiveness is a choice you make for yourself. It is about taking responsibility for how you feel. The choice to forgive renews your heart and refreshes your soul. It is your path to inner peace and personal power. Forgiving yourself and forgiving others require non-judgment and objectivity; learning to separate the person from the behavior. You can learn how to shift your perspective so that your heart opens and softens through empathy and compassion. I believe that people are fundamentally good. Notice what you see and feel when you look at a newborn baby — innocence, vulnerability, and natural tendency to trust and connect. The conditioning in your early, formative years has significant influence over your choices and actions. The behaviors typically replayed as adults are the ones most familiar simply from being a product of your environment, hence the saying, "children learn what they live."

BEYOND THE TALK

We can talk and talk and talk about what is wrong with our lives. The energy behind the words and feelings reinforces that which we do not desire. Therefore, we must go beyond the talk, beyond the complaining, beyond the repetitive behaviors of reenacting and replaying the same old painful memories over and over again in order to resolve inner conflict, in order to find peace. We must evolve to a higher level; reinforce that which we want to create in our lives with constructive language, intention, and imagination.

In a quiet space…Affirm your heart's sincere intention and your heart's deepest desire --- open and allow for this engaging and clarifying process to emerge from a place of appreciation and acceptance; a place that allows you to unconditionally be with "what is" in the moment, regardless of situation or circumstance.

We can be in a crowded room and feel alone. We can be alone yet feel the presence of warmth and love in our lives, and support and power in our being. Know that we are all connected to each other and know that we are all connected to a source greater than ourselves. It is important to recognize how we choose to view ourselves, our situations, as well as the meaning we attach to all of it. The meaning we give to a situation gives rise to an emotion, and the emotion can be constructive or destructive. The rising emotion can be outwardly displayed with abruptness, harshness, aggressiveness, resistance, or violence, and it can also be inwardly displayed with the same intensity. The same emotion, if we choose, can have a more positive effect, where there is a sense of calm, peace, objectivity, empathy, enthusiasm, or passion. Regardless of the circumstance, the origin of our behavior is from within. Our emotions and behaviors are a reflection of our inner view or perspective, which is founded on past experiences, learned behaviors, and core beliefs.

HANGING ON TO PAINFUL REMINDERS

Each day has within it, new opportunities, new experiences, possibly new hurts and disappointments, so *why do we choose to carry new hurts on top of earlier hurts?* The way we process and handle our painful experiences has cumulative effects, building one on top of the other. The burden can become great, the load very heavy and overwhelming, ultimately rendering us weary and sick.

- *What is there to gain from holding on to painful memories as if they were priceless possessions?*
- *How do we let go and allow ourselves to learn from painful experiences, open our hearts to compassion and forgiveness, to ultimately feel a sense of ease and well-being?*

The things we do or do not do provide us directly or indirectly with some kind of gain, some kind of reinforcement, whether we are aware of it or not, whether it is beneficial or harmful. I refer to this as a "secondary gain." It is one thing to keep memorabilia for the joyful reminders of meaningful experiences and precious moments, for the warm fuzzy feelings they provide . . . *but what happens when we decide to hold on to things from the past that were traumatic, painful, destructive – things that trigger memories or remind us of times we would rather forget, wish that never took place? Why would we do this?*

You may find value in holding on to painful reminders. There is validation of wrongdoing, proof of an undeniable event, a reason to stay where you are; to stay angry, depressed, anxious, or frustrated instead of working to move through it, rise up and out of it. There is reinforcement of the negative experience that gives you a fall back, a legitimate excuse for your pain, your lack of happiness, and your lack of success; a reason not to take full responsibility for your life's outcomes. Recognize the burden that such an activity places on your ability to move forward in your life, your ability to forgive yourself or your oppressor, the self-imposed limits you set on yourself, the energy you use to stay stuck in time.

Ask yourself:

- *Why are you giving life to the very things that caused you the greatest struggle, anguish, and strife?*
- *When are you going to recognize that you are depriving yourself of a full and complete life, that every time you choose to revisit your painful reminders for a "reassurance check," you are actually withdrawing from your happiness and fulfillment account?*

You slowly deplete and deprive yourself of wonderful and prosperous opportunities. You affirm and reaffirm for yourself false truths. You invalidate your self-worth, you render yourself undeserving, unworthy, and unable; you self-sabotage your life and your future. You choose to give your power away. You choose to revisit your past because of your attachment to it. You develop a sense of security with your painful memories. To truly heal and move forward in your life, you have to decide to change this painful yet familiar model, be willing to let go, to lovingly and respectfully detach from that which does not serve your highest good and is not in alignment with your higher purpose. This means you no longer give yourself permission to revisit or reactivate those memories. Recognize your attachment and your comfort level with this false sense of security. Make a decision to acknowledge your true self, give value to your life's experiences.

Ask yourself:

- *What does it really mean to me to hold on to these memories?*
- *What good is it doing for me?*
- *What effect does it have on me and on the people in my life?*
- *Am I willing to release these ties in order to grow myself into the person I know I can be?*
- *Am I willing to accept myself, forgive myself, and forgive others so I can free myself up to live fully?*
- *Am I willing to trust again and open myself to learning from my experiences?*

BEGIN TO LOVE, FORGIVE, AND ACCEPT YOURSELF AS YOU ARE

Discover, embrace, and root to your source of life, your Divine grounding connection. This magnificent source of life is ever-loving, forgiving, and nurturing. Close your eyes and sense your light energy's presence and vibration flowing throughout your bloodstream, flowing deep within and throughout every cell of your being, and abundantly flowing, penetrating, and filling your heart. Deeply sense and connect within, to the essence of your existence, appreciating and honoring your inherent value and worthiness; recognizing your ability to generously love and be loved. With this awakened sense and appreciation, you may begin to explore life with a new perspective, opening your heart and soul to the goodness that exists all around you. This way of living takes practice and requires your commitment to being a person of authentic influence who can show love and be loved without fear of the world's reactions. Presenting the best of yourself at all times is not always easy to do. For this reason, you must continuously practice loving self-talk and display loving acts of kindness towards yourself and others at every opportunity.

OPEN YOUR HEART IN JOYFUL SERVICE

Life offers us opportunities to connect with one another everywhere we go. I believe the greatest human desire and ultimate life lesson is realized in the *experience* of engaging and connecting authentically and unconditionally from the heart. Let us learn to freely open ourselves to making heart-to-heart connections, connections that transmit an inherently pure, divine message—a message so powerful it conveys without words, "I care about you, I accept you, I trust you, you matter, and you are loved just because . . ."

- *What is more meaningful than this realization?*
- *How does one make this type of connection without misinterpretation and judgment both from an internal perspective and external perspective?*

Learning to appreciate heart-to-heart connections has far reaching and transformative effects on our lives. These kinds of connections embrace the essence of life and the human being that represents life. Recognize at the onset that fear and insecurity are at the root of misinterpretation and judgment. For whatever given reason, we are so far removed from our true, authentic self. We live with the notion that we should be able to fully control our lives and our environment. To a limited extent we have control of external factors but the greatest control we have is on our internal responses and corresponding behaviors. We tend to feed our ego, develop our identity, our self-worth, and our viewpoint on life through successful "ownership" or "acquisition" of whatever is physically accessible and tangible. Example of this sort of ownership-acquisition is gained through relationships, roles, titles, or material possessions. We engage in needy and desperate behaviors due to an inner sense of void, lack, and deprivation. We demonstrate excessiveness in wanting to have, to own, to know; a desperateness for an explanation or answers for the infamous "why me" questions. The lack of individual and collective awareness of these behaviors permits for and perpetuates continued fear-based interpretations and reactions leading to unfulfilled hopes and dreams, and revisiting of pain, heartache, despair, and disappointment.

- *How do we behave in our personal relationships and in our day-to-day interactions?*

As a society, we spend a great deal of time role playing and labeling. We view ourselves and each other through titles, labels, illnesses, or perhaps particular situations. This, for the most part, can become our personal identity and the roles we start to play. Depending on the situation or environment we are in, our communication and interaction are filtered through these various roles; there is an unspoken expectation of how communication should flow. There is a hierarchical type of role playing that limits our ability to make true, unconditional heart-to-heart connections. Unconsciously, we set up barriers and lead with judgment and preconceived notions. Much of our conversation is tailored for appropriateness based on our perceptions of these identified roles. As I continue to learn and grow through my training and experiences, I gain a sense of knowing that what I share is truly possible and available for you to experience. With awareness, you can make a shift into consciousness. Consciousness opens you to a sense of freedom, peace, and purpose, which delights in the interconnectedness of your being one with all life; lifting, appreciating, and uniting through love and compassion. This way of being makes room for authentic interaction without fear and judgment or comparison and competition.

Remember . . .

FORGIVENESS is our

prescription for salvation —

the salve for our soul —

the balm with which we soothe our open wounds.

Forgiveness is your RELEASE valve!
- Releases the ties that bind
- Releases the grip of pain and heartache...
- Releases the strongholds that keep you stuck and keep you from healing

Forgiveness is a CHOICE you make on your behalf; for your well-being and happiness!

"If we really want to love we must learn how to forgive."

~Mother Teresa

IV
SELF-IMAGE

PRESERVING DIGNITY AND SELF-RESPECT

The value of our image on the outside is playing a greater role in why we do the things we do. There is significant attention being placed on the external image, on how we look, our facial appearance and body shape, instead of finding value with the internal image and person on the inside. The pressure to keep up with the look is not only financially costly, but costly to the development of character and self-worth. Many of our feelings and behaviors arise out of our image and perception of self. We are willing to take risk with our health in order to improve our image. The commonplace practice of plastic surgery to correct minor imperfections and flaws, to enhance our appearance, is starting earlier with our youth. This external "fix" or "correction" has become the vehicle to improving our self-image. How we see ourselves on the outside does affect how we feel on the inside, however, we are way out of balance. We focus more attention on keeping up with the external image to overcompensate for what is missing on the inside. The internal image is temporarily pacified and satisfied by the overflow from the attention given to the external image; however, there does come a point in time when our internal image desires to be recognized and valued. We may have unconsciously experienced a period of miscommunication or disconnection between the outer and inner self-image. The dynamics of a healthy body image in balance is represented as an integrated and an interdependent fluid "whole" comprised of mind, body, spirit, and emotions. All parts relate and interact, so it is important to keep lines of communication open, allowing for information to flow. The opposite of this is stagnation. It is important to recognize that when we embody this physiological state of flow or stagnation, it is communicated and reflected in our "presence," referring to an energetic or resonant state of embodiment; meaning how we show up in the world.

Many people who live with the fear of rejection also tend to reject themselves. It is important that we take good care of ourselves, feel good about ourselves, and remain in alignment with our true, authentic nature. We can create and nurture a balanced, positive self-image when we begin with a healthy sense of self-worth and self-respect. When we continually look to the outward appearance as our gauge for self-worth, self-appeal, and self-acceptance, this ultimately becomes our value system. This type of system many times becomes a burden to maintain, leading to extreme, costly, careless, or desperate behaviors and a limited, false perception of self. The true value of who we are on the inside becomes negligible. Who you are on the inside should have much greater importance and value because it is the real you. It is important to believe that who you truly are on the inside will carry you through life regardless of your circumstances. Developing your value system speaks loudly to your character, to your integrity — to the person you know you really are on the inside. Self-love and acceptance helps you feel confident, be much more authentic and genuine, and have a positive overall view of yourself and life. Keep in mind that when you scrutinize or judge the appearance of other people, you often consciously or unconsciously look for the same or similar things to judge or scrutinize in yourself.

- *What are you saying and doing to appeal to the inner image in a much deeper, longer lasting manner to derive a good sense of self and a positive self-image?*

As parents, raising children today is quite the challenge. We have the world of television, internet, radio, magazines, and billboards sending messages to our children that image is everything. At home, parents have to counteract this bombardment. This constant exposure does not allow our children to fully develop from the inside because the focus and attraction on outward appearances is magnified. The development of a healthy outlook, an intrinsic value system, positive self-esteem and self-respect, and the interest in pursuing higher education take a backseat.

We can observe the behavior of people of all ages, especially women and young adolescent girls, comparing themselves and belittling others based on their appearances and their material possessions. We see that parents are being pressured by their children to conform, and parents are living through their children. Parents are buying into the outer image hype to the extent of putting their children at risk with surgical procedures for the sake of appearances. Television is regularly portraying the glamour of lifestyles that are extravagant along with having expectations that are extravagant, both of which are misleading our youth. The message being sent is that we deserve to have what we want when we want it. At home and as a society at large, we should be teaching our youth what it takes to earn their way to success, help them develop a work ethic and appreciation for what it takes to earn these niceties. These valuable teachings are not being conveyed through the media and oftentimes not being conveyed at home. We are seeing the collapse of an internal value system, which includes self-respect, self-esteem, self-worth, self-discipline, self-love, self-appreciation, self-confidence, a positive self-image, and secure self-identity. The way we look at life and how we see ourselves is all wrapped up in a facade. It is our role as parents and as a society to be positive role models, to teach our children to love and respect themselves and to love and respect others— to help them foster a sense of self-worth and self-discipline, and develop a value system. We should lead by example to help our children understand the value of respect, appreciation, consideration, and contribution; demonstrate examples of kindness, working together, giving back, and providing excellent and meaningful service. These are the life-enhancing fundamentals that lend to a thriving, cohesive, and supportive society, which reinforce the very core of where we all truly live, in our inner child's heart.

THOUGHTS ON SELF-IMAGE: ME, MYSELF, AND I

The image you have of yourself has significant influence on your decisions, your outlook on your abilities and your opportunities, your sense of security, and ultimately, your life as a whole. What you think and feel about yourself is foundational; it is the canvas on which you design your life. Your self-image affects you positively or negatively, leading you into behaviors and feelings towards yourself that are either supporting you or bringing you down: self-denial, self-loathing, self-sabotage, self-annihilation, or self-love, self-worth, self-affirmation, self-appreciation, and self-respect. If your life should change suddenly or unexpectedly from what you have known, find your way back to your heart. Connect with your core values and deeply sense who you are, why you are here, and what life means to you. Recognize that how you feel about yourself will play out in how others see and feel about you. There is a direct relationship in how you see yourself and, subsequently, how others behave towards you. If you have a negative self-image, your view and expectation of yourself is lessened and the view and expectation others have of you will be lessened as well. Many times, people will take advantage of your insecurity and you may do things to fit in, to please, or to avoid pain or embarrassment. You tend to reach for the immediate pleasure and gratification of the moment. Please do not make decisions when you feel desperate. Deep down, a decision from the energy of desperation will usually go against your better judgment and result in an undesired outcome. When your image is positive, your expectation of yourself is raised, and this will affect the expectation and perception others will have of you. Your life has great meaning and purpose. Transform your beliefs about who you are. You are responsible for your life! You hold the reins! Take full ownership for all of your experiences. Stop the excuses, stop the blaming, and stop the complaining. Make a decision to live your life on purpose with purpose. Live courageously and compassionately through your heart. Develop character strength and integrity and build trust and self-esteem through your commitment to self-love, self-honor, self-respect, and self-discipline. As you persevere with these heart-focused and self-affirming actions, you will discover yourself on the path to personal growth and transformation and ultimately self-mastery.

Look in the Mirror and Affirm:

"I am loving"

"I am lovable"

"I am worthy"

"I am well and able"

"I am equipped"

"I am happy, healthy, and strong"

It is not our

charge to

make others

see the light,

instead,

BE the LIGHT!

V
CULTIVATING COMPASSION

SELF-COMPASSION

Compassion is an archway that opens to your heart's path for inner healing, resolving conflict, and restoring relationships. The interweaving of empathy and heartfelt intention for a positive, constructive and peaceful way forward complements the process of cultivating compassion. Imagine that once you step through this archway you are surrounded by the fresh air of appreciation and acceptance — feel the infusion of appreciation and acceptance gently permeating each and every cell, acknowledging all that you have been through. Compassion offers you a perspective that expands your view of what is possible and expands your heart's capacity for self-love and forgiveness, as well as love and forgiveness of others and a healthier overall view of a situation or experience. You may weep along this path, deeply feeling your heart's desires for peace and serenity, harmony and genuine relief. Sincerely open to your feelings. Give yourself permission to feel whatever you feel, without judgment, aversion, resistance, blame or shame. Compassion helps you to be deeply present with your emotions, especially with painful and highly charged emotions like grief, anger or rage. Self-compassion is like welcoming in a close and trustworthy friend to sit with you, listen to you, allowing you to express what you feel, recognizing your sincere efforts, and acknowledging your pain and struggle. Your willingness and patience to simply be with your pain and suffering help you to cultivate compassion.

COMPASSION FOR OTHERS

When we hold others on the hook for wrongdoing or hurtful behaviors, we are also holding ourselves on the hook. The process of allowing compassion to infuse into our cells and into our being cultivates an inner state of peace and tranquility. This is the environment that helps us make room for resolving deeply painful emotions. It does not condone or deny the behavior or action that caused the pain, it simply offers a space to rest peacefully with all of what we feel, and this helps to dissipate, dissolve, and take the "charge" off a highly charged emotion. This path simultaneously nurtures as it offers us a way to grow through our experiences and provides us another lens in which to view and renew from our most powerful and purest foundation...the Divine presence of unconditional love and acceptance of ourselves and life itself. We typically think of compassion as a warm and friendly feeling, however, compassion is also an inner experience as it is a loving and courageous presence and a powerful resource that affects our physiology and biochemistry. Research at the Institute of HeartMath® (www.heartmath.org), on the physiological and psychological effects of compassion and anger found that sincere, heart-focused feelings boosted the immune system whereas negative emotions could suppress the immune response nearly six hours after the emotional experience.[4] In the book, Buddha's Brain, neuroscience supports that the practice of cultivating compassion is actively working in one's brain, helping to strengthen the circuitry in the regions of the anterior cingulated cortex and insula.[5] (p.155) This *body* of knowledge confirms that we can effect positive change in our lives, in our relationships, and in our health; it supports that it is healthy for us to practice living from the unconditional goodness of our hearts, showing genuine concern and kindness for others as well as for ourselves. The mindful practice and presence of kindness can become automatic and will naturally and subtly weave into our thoughts, actions, voices, and into our being. It is important for us to pay attention to what is happening within our bodies during conversations, observations, and interactions. The ability to differentiate between the thoughts and feelings that emerge in our internal environment with respect to the thoughts, feelings, and actions of others in our external environment will support our ability to practice empathy and compassion and help us establish and maintain healthy and respectable boundaries with our relationships.

REDEFINING SENSITIVITY AND VULNERABILITY

- *How do you currently define sensitivity and vulnerability?*
- *What are your beliefs about being sensitive and vulnerable?*

Entering through the archway of compassion opens us up to preexisting beliefs and perceptions. Recognizing our definition or interpretation of words as they translate to our feelings is essential to our ability to cultivate compassion, to forgive, heal, and transform our lives. Once through this archway, there is an invitation awaiting us to explore a level of sensitivity and vulnerability, which we may not feel so warm and receptive to initially. The familiar language and conditioned beliefs around sensitivity and vulnerability may feel emotionally or mentally disruptive and "charged," or provoke a perceived sense of volatility. The internal sense of vastness and raw openness may have us feeling fragile and uneasy, even somewhat anxious because of our prior experiences and expectations. However, when we choose to explore this precious space of sensitivity and vulnerability, we begin to consider another possibility; a shift in our prior working definition emerges. The subtle unveiling and realization of sensitivity and vulnerability in their pure essence as a powerful platform where we can rest and restore, but also where we are acutely aware of our relationships to people, external situations and events and how they affect us or move us on the inside becomes a life-changing awareness and practice. This awareness actually serves as a *field of awareness,* our heart field expanding its outreach and influence. The heart field establishes a kind of sacred boundary that has intelligent "feelers" tuned in to both our inner and outer world. It is in and through this space we are able to gauge what is happening in both worlds simultaneously. It is through the mindful and intentional practice of accessing this profound field of knowledge and awareness, we are able to authentically engage in heartfelt communication and make choices and decisions from acknowledging and honoring what is true and meaningful in our lives.

- *Can you feel the subtle strength and awareness inherent to sensitivity and vulnerability?*

His Holiness, Tenzin Gyatso, the fourteenth Dalai Lama, stated in the article, Compassion and the Individual, "For a person who cherishes compassion and love, the practice of tolerance is essential, and for that, an enemy is indispensable. So we should feel grateful to our enemies, for it is they who can best help us develop a tranquil mind!"[6]

"PATIENCE is a Powerful Principle,
Virtue, and PRACTICE!"

MIRROR OF TRUTH
Reflections of the Heart

Collection of My Heart Inspired Writings...

The Power of the
Spoken Word...

We are to be mindful of the
words we choose when
speaking to or about another,
for they are in turn the same
words we speak to ourselves.

~

Look into the eyes of a child,
a loved one, or a stranger
perhaps and SEE yourself...

DOSE OF DEBORAH:
A Spoon Full of Inspiration and Insight

I offer you inspiration and insights to increase self-aware-
ness, self-love and self-acceptance leading to self-growth,
personal transformation and fulfillment...

It is my intention to provide you with content that is
thoughtful, educational, engaging, inspirational, and empow-
ering. As you read through this book, may you find support
and encouragement; receive food for thought that can assist
you in gaining a new perspective on your life experiences.

There is a great deal of pain today. I desire to help you tap
into another way to look at your life experiences; find a way
to appreciate your experiences. Your increased awareness
and insight will contribute to your personal growth and have
rippling effects on all of your relationships, especially the
relationship you have with yourself. I feel that if you connect
with me in any way or resonate with any part of what has been
written, you make available that space within you that says
yes...yes to an opportunity and to the possibility of a deeper
connection to yourself....to find healing, passion, and purpose
in your life. I believe in possibilities, I believe in miracles, and
I believe in YOU!

We affect each other's lives.

RETURN TO SELF

*I desire to live freely and fully—this being the highest expression of my Self. Little did I know that the truth of an ongoing struggle was due to a missing piece, "my peace," a part lost and denied by me. I awakened to a deeper knowing truth through a meditative practice of neutral and non-judgmental presence. This practice revealed to me, the sacrifice made of losing what was part of me, would never again be a part of me—separated from me, as I believed, that lost part of me would no longer be free. Freedom held at bay, sabotaging day-by-day, was the way I coped as I mourned my loss. The realization of "fullness" would never be, until I recognized the true loss was me. My **Self** abandoned and sacrificed as a way to cope with pain and sorrow which I unknowingly invited into tomorrow. The piece and peace that longed to return would do so upon my opening to unconditional love and acceptance, releasing the shame and the blame that had me confined. I say to thee,"Come home, I long to be, re-connected with you that is detached from me. Return to me now, fill my heart and **hole** with love and valor, and make me **whole** with God's grace and honor. I realize now the "me" seeks "we" to BE free to live in Harmony."*

LOVE AND ACCEPT YOURSELF
AS YOU ARE

*In Honor of who you are and all that you've been through...
I am grateful for where you are now, this very moment. I say
to you that it is through the heart you have been hurt and it is
through the heart you will find healing!*

<u>*Poem*</u>*: In Me I See...Possibility...*

I am fragile, I am bold, in silence I suffer, my woes yet
untold. The depths of my despair SO weigh on my heart and
soul! I cry inside and cry out loud for no one to hear or care
for I fear—judgment and blame, that little ole game we play
with each other when we our true selves are a reflection of the
same. The same desires, needs, and hopes, we seek acceptance
and love as life unfolds. The regularity of doubt, discourage-
ment, and depression I do not tell, the strongholds of shame,
blame and guilt I know all too well. So many mistakes, so
many failures, how does one recover, how does one override
the pain and misery felt deep, deep inside—the traumas and
dramas I have no one to confide...

So tired from exhaustion and depression, keep denying
truthful expression, the suppression of anger and possibly
rage, feeling stifled and caged! I love to laugh although I

often cry, the desire to thrive keeps me going, keeps me alive. Struggling and striving to pull myself up, to pull myself out— for this pain I feel, the sense of overwhelming doubt eats at my soul, eats at my heart, and sometimes feels like I am falling apart. The turmoil inside begins to erupt and override my efforts to suppress and further lock down denied. My heart is open although it still hurts and cries, the echoes of sadness and madness, makes me want to fly—fly high and far yonder where no one will hear or see, the despair and pain I feel yet I still ponder...

I feel like a fragile baby, at the same time like a wounded soldier, a tender-hearted warrior who has started on the path of great wonder. The quiet yet vulnerable state in which I live somehow offers me solace, a safe haven inviting me to forgive. So how do I move forward and rise out of despair, for I care most deeply, I desire to share...

My answer revealed, that I now see, is God's pure and unbridled love for me. An unshakeable faith and courage subtly moves in and through me, filling my heart and engaging my soul with possibility...

As I gratefully open my heart to compassion beyond compare, to share for all who need to hear, a voice of hope and triumph that your life matters and I truly care. A voice whispers, "Angel of Mercy there's no shame or blame, love unconditionally, and please stay in the game. The game of life, you play to win—let your game begin, as you now recognize the magnificence within."

Love and Gratitude

GROWING "IN" TO OURSELVES

We often refer to the aging process as growing up. As we go through life, our experiences are to teach us and grow us; through the best and worst of our life experiences and all that is in between, we are expected to mature—gaining wisdom and insight from the variety of lessons life offers. When challenged by life's experiences, the way to truly rise and triumph, overcome and move forward is to grow inward; developing a closer relationship with ourselves, getting to know and love ourselves, gaining objectivity and clarity. Learning to appreciate ALL of our experiences will assist in boosting self-confidence, self-esteem, and self-worth.

Rise in Your Greatness *You are born great, however, many of you play small. You are born with amazing potential; unique gifts and talents to share. It's up to you to realize and appreciate your uniquely YOU greatness. Life's experiences may have you feeling less than, not deserving, fearful, lacking confidence or self-worth. As long as there is breath in your body, a new experience is possible... What kind of experiences do you desire to create in your life?*

When you rise in your life, you can assist others to rise in theirs. When you do less than you are capable of, you have less to contribute. This "less" not only affects others, but is a direct feedback to you. You are your own worst enemy or your best friend. It's up to you to help yourself, to see your-self through your child's heart...curious, creative, and open. Are you ready to feel different, do differently, and do better? Decide now and commit to your decision. Your life matters and you are worth it.

REAL OR IMAGINED, WHAT YOU PERCEIVE TO BE TRUE BECOMES YOUR REALITY

I was deeply saddened by the news of a tragedy involving a teenage girl in high school who chose to end her life, and the rippling effects of shock and devastation felt by her family, friends, and peers. Adding insult to injury was the response from some of her peers who chose to judge and criticize her, express harsh opinions, instead of choosing to show empathy or compassion. As a mother of two teenage daughters, this tragic incident prompted a heartfelt discussion within our family.

Let us take a moment in quiet thought and reflection to send our prayers and sentiments to families that have just lost a child, grandchild, parent, sibling, spouse, partner, relative, friend, co-worker, colleague; and prayers and sentiments for those without family or friends...

We all affect each other with our comments and criticisms. A little kindness and compassion can go a long way. We do not know the details or depth of the thoughts and feelings of others to the extent that one would consider ending his or her life.

What was this young girl's perception of reality that she saw no better option than to end her life? How do her family and close friends view this situation?

What is your Perception of Reality? This has nothing to do with being right or wrong. It is how you see yourself and your situation.

Do you recognize where your viewpoints originate? Why are some people quick to judge others and their behaviors? How does it make you feel when you judge someone? How would you feel to have people judge you? Can you open yourself to appreciate a point of view that is different to yours?

How do you view your life today? Your state of mind matters. Stress, emotional distress, and depression are a few considerations that contribute to our outlook. Our emotional and spiritual health contribute to our physical health and our outlook on life. As a society, we can assist and support each other. We must become more mindful and considerate during our interactions with one another.

YOU ARE NOT ALONE!

We Are On This Journey Together! *Our individual lives contribute to the greater "Whole." Every one of us has something unique and special to offer. We mirror for each other with every encounter and interaction—the inner perspective revealed through comments and criticisms; compliments or complaints. The more secure we are on the inside and the better we feel about ourselves, the nicer we tend to be.* **"Happy people don't say mean things."** *When we take better care of ourselves, we are able to take better care of others, hence the term "Caregiver." We are ALL caregivers. Everywhere we go, we are to "CARE" for one another...to be mindful and considerate of our fellow brothers and sisters.*

As we care for others, it is essential that we also care for ourselves. We are to recognize our strengths and weaknesses and seek to gain an appreciation for the lessons offered through our life experiences. We are to accept ourselves as we are and open ourselves to believing in possibilities beyond measure, beyond our greatest imagination, and even beyond rational thought. It is important that we take personal responsibility for the choices and decisions we make. We can help ourselves by establishing a personal honor code, which includes healthy personal boundaries and healthy, nurturing habits that lend to life-enhancing relationships, especially the relationship we have with our precious self.

How do we care for ourselves? We care for ourselves through Self-Love, Self-Appreciation, and Self-Awareness: Be Aware of how you treat yourself; become conscious and mindful of your attitude, behaviors, influences, perceptions, and beliefs. Be your own Best Friend. PAUSE, take a Deep Breath and "BE" where you are–as you are–this very moment. Be Present with the Moments of your life; be Quiet and Listen. There is a STILL, small VOICE inside speaking to you, desiring your attention, desiring to connect and communicate with you. Be Kind and Patient with yourself. OPEN yourself to Growing and Flowing... Appreciating "All that is," all that has been, and all that is yet to be. ALLOW your HEART to expand its CAPACITY to Love Unconditionally, Forgive, Heal, Renew, and Restore.

Every day is its own day:

As we awaken to each new day, let us briefly REFLECT... let us take time for Quiet INTROSPECTION...

What are you grateful for? Is there anything new you have discovered about yourself? Are you listening to that STILL small voice seeking your attention? What has this year revealed to you? What realizations have you made? What contributions have you made with your time, energy, talent, resources, etc.? Have you grown as a person, moved forward or moved through any major challenge or adversity? What life lessons have you learned? What goals have you accomplished? What are you bringing forward into the New Year?

In any moment, we can choose to RESOLVE and

EVOLVE...   beyond what we currently know, beyond what we thought was possible... What are your dreams, goals, and desires? What are your abilities, talents, interests, etc.? Are there any areas with which you desire support or assistance? Do you have a support network? Who is in your support network? What IN you is seeking to come forward; to be expressed through you? Are you willing to grow and stretch yourself? Are you ready for change? Are you truly committed to your success, to feeling better, to doing better, to doing differently?

YOUR BODY IS A MASTERPIECE, A SYMPHONY, A MAGNIFICENT CREATION

We are energy, we are light, and we are music in motion— a harmonic expression...we flow, we resonate, we radiate, we express...

Our bodies communicate with us. The terms we use to describe our lives, our situations, or our circumstances, mirror what is happening on the inside of our bodies. The tensions, restrictions, adhesions, compensations, holding patterns, and disease processes that occur inside our bodies due to injury, neglect, abuse, and trauma whether physical or emotional, have us languaging in a way to bring our attention inward; to bring our attention to what we are really feeling on a much deeper core level. Most of us are not aware of this until our attention is directly or indirectly brought to it.

The energy we expend to compensate, hide, resist, brace, hold on to, and harbor, is significant. Its effects can be direct, indirect, and subtle on our health and well-being both for the short term and long term without our awareness. When we are out of alignment within our bodies, out of sync, not flowing freely and comfortably, this has effects on how we view our world outside our bodies...how we view our lives, our situations, and our relationships.

Our cells, tissues, nervous system, and all our systems are constantly interacting and responding to our experiences; responding to our environment both on the inside and the outside of our bodies.

I ask you now to give your attention to the light presence that is within you; the light that is you, that radiates through you and beyond you. Raise your vibration to align with your highest self, your higher intuitive knowing self, the self that longs and cries for your attention. Embrace and appreciate all that makes you unique.

May you find peace within.

With gratitude for the Divine inner guidance that is within us all.

YOUR LIFE IS A MIRACLE—YOUR ABILITIES ARE AMAZING!

Several mornings ago, I found myself tossing and turning to get comfortable. At some point, I began to have thoughts of my patient who just recently came into my care. Although half awake, half asleep, I was acknowledging my ability to move and reposition at will. In a matter of a few seconds, my thoughts then turned to the life altering affects of my patient's injuries that have him lying in bed without the ability to do such a seemingly simple function as turning on his side. I recalled the concern reflected in his eyes, "How did I get myself into this?" "Why did this happen?" "What's to come of my life?"

Recovery from a spinal cord injury is a process...moment by moment. The initial shock after an accident, the initial fear and uncertainty of survival, the subsequent fear and uncertainty of recovery are real and immediate. The life altering changes in functionality are BOLDLY evident. The body you once knew has drastically changed and is now unfamiliar.

It is so important we take time to appreciate the abilities we have. The ability to breathe, think, interact, eat, drink, taste, smell, touch, feel, move, walk , talk, control our bowel and bladder...the ability to be independent, get up and go where we want to and when we want to, to drive, to travel, etc. are things we must be mindful of and take care of. Appreciate the moment. We must take time each day to express gratitude for all of our abilities and opportunities.

Every day is a gift, a blessing, and a present. Stay PRESENT!

There is a SHIFT taking place in our internal and external environments

People want desperately to feel...to feel connected to self and to life itself...to feel engaged in life!

For several decades now, as I use my youth as a period of reference, I have noticed a slow disconnect over time–a disconnect from self and others. We have seen a significant increase in the dreaded "D" list: despair, depression, devastation, doubt, divorce, disease, delusion, disillusionment, drugs, "drinking", and death. What has happened to our neighborhoods, or should I say the sense of neighborhood and the sense of community? The hierarchy of respect we used to show as kids when talking with adults, referring to them as "Mr. and Mrs." is a thing of the past. The overall regard for authority has greatly diminished. There is increased force and brutality as a means of communication.

We have manifested into a culture of high tech-low touch communication. This has influenced the devaluing of life and of SELF; has shown to increase stress and stress related illnesses, and has contributed to decreased self-esteem and decreased job satisfaction. There is greater emphasis on keeping up the "image" which has affected our ability to authentically communicate because of this external "mask" effect. There is an underlying fear of not being good enough, pretty enough, or worthy enough, so individually and collectively, we have learned how to compensate for this "lack." This compensation, however, does not truly fill the void of what really matters, the love and connections we desire in our lives, the feelings of self-worth and self-confidence that enable us to walk and talk with authenticity. Our abilities, behaviors, and outcomes are a result of our thoughts, beliefs, perceptions, and attitudes.

Currently, in our daily lives, we are seeing heightened states of frustration and intolerances, lack of compassion and conscientiousness, desperate acts for attention, increased acts of violence and more... However, what I am gradually noticing through conversation and observation is a desire to return to feeling connected, starting with the connection to self. Through the chaos, a SHIFT is taking place, a desire to stop feeling sick and tired of being sick and tired. There is a growing awareness that change is necessary. The heart is calling for our attention, is longing for true connection—that connection to self which allows us to discover our personal truths, authentically connect with one another and connect with the very essence of life itself.

YOUR AUTHENTIC TRUTH REMAINS
THE SAME

At four years old, she was told something that became her belief, her truth…

At any age, we all seek a fundamental truth, a truth we initially look for outside ourselves, a truth we derive from others to validate our lives; the truth of unconditional acceptance and validation of our being, of our worthiness. The truth is we know our truth, but often get disconnected from our truth.

I had the most amazing soulful connection with an 80-year-old woman this past week in the therapy clinic; one of the most inspiring and enlightening experiences of my life. She has been questioning the reasons for her struggles over the past few decades of her life, although she was very successful in her business before retirement. In my brief observation and through conversation, I sensed she had been allowing herself to die slowly and painfully with the aging process; dying to Self; denial of Self; deprecation and destruction of Self; denying herself the joy that stems from living her passion, a passion that moves her spirit and fills her soul.

She questioned, what was the point anymore, what was the purpose to her life? She questioned what it was to have faith or to "trust in the process." She said that getting old was painful and nobody really cared.

For years, she has had difficulty sleeping and feels depressed when awake. One would think she was simply depressed, which can occur with aging. She recently had surgery and her body was healing, but in addition to the physical healing, she was dealing with many emotions that were surfacing, causing feelings of unrest and uncertainty.

I asked her what she enjoyed doing. She told me she spends time with her family. She has been married for over sixty years, and has children, grandchildren, and great grandchildren. She told me she looks at old pictures of herself and sees a young girl who is no longer present. That profound comment immediately caught my heart's attention. I looked directly into her eyes and said, "That girl is still very present, she still lives inside you, she has never left you, it is you who have left her, denied her." She looked at me—there was a moment of silence. As I continued to talk with her, I found out her interests and talents, which were indeed, her passion...poetry and art, painting and drawing. "How beautiful," I remarked. I shared that this natural ability to creatively express, was a gift, uniquely hers.

"What's the point," she said, "No one cares about this kind of stuff anymore. They are too busy with other things, with gadgets and interests elsewhere. I don't want to bring people down with my views on life. My views are not like yours."

I asked her how she felt when she used to write poetry and paint. She said she felt alive, she was inspired. The creativity came through her onto paper and onto canvas. I gently brought to her attention that while she was expecting others to find value with her inspired works of art, she was not appreciating and valuing these works for herself.

Although her outlook was pessimistic and doubtful, it was her reality being expressed, her feelings and perspective that had me intrigued and inspired. I was greatly inspired by our connection, the enriching content of our heart and soulful communication. She expressed feeling inspired by my outlook but said she could not connect with it. I challenged her on this, for I knew on a deeper level, she was truly moved and engaged but was resisting her own authentic truth... for the truth that she has known and lived with for eight decades, a truth told to her in her youth by her father, a person she dearly loved and respected, had prevailed throughout her life. I asked her to consider that the intention of our meeting was to bring attention to her symptoms of restlessness and depression as a message from her body, to open her to a new perspective that the possibility her truth did not match her father's truth. She acknowledged me with a look, neither denying nor confirming the possibility...

My hope for capturing and re-creating the essence of this experience is for you to personally experience each insightful and inspiring moment. Are you able to sense the intimacy and vulnerability of this extraordinary exchange? What do you feel will follow from this interaction? Does this remarkable story invite any feelings of your own to surface? Does it penetrate deep within, at a level you may not have been aware of before reading this? Are you moved in any way?

What are you seeking in your life? What really matters to

you? What brings you joy and happiness—what inspires you, makes your heart sing? Do you acknowledge yourself, your deeper authentic Self that you know intimately or are you afraid to open up and reveal yourself for fear of misunderstandings, judgment, criticism, or ridicule? Are you wrestling with or resisting your truth, your authentic truth? Are you questioning something someone told you, a belief that you made your own? Are you revisited by your conscience, your intuitive guide?

At any age, our authentic truth remains the same. Deep within our core is a belief that we inherently know as our truth, an inner wisdom with which we came into this world. We are born with a magnificent sense of the truth of who we are—this is our foundational truth, our unique truth embedded and encoded within us that guides our growth and expansion, offering insight and stability in our lives. Yet, sadly, we lose touch with our truth; we "seemingly" separate from our deeper knowing Self. We spend our lives mirroring and modeling for each other, creating perceptions of false truths based on our conditioned beliefs and perspectives from our life experiences, thus creating lifelong impressions in our minds and hearts. Such intimate influences and connections contribute to our current beliefs and behaviors, and even our physiology. It is a practice and a discipline, once we become aware, to learn how to trust, to not fear or resist our inner knowing and guidance. As I learn to expand my awareness, to be a presence of unconditional love and acceptance, I find myself engaging and listening with an open-hearted presence to what is present, a subtle knowing beyond words… I truly believe our essence is love. We embody a Divine Spirit, that which is love of the purest kind. This loving Spirit nurtures us, keeps us "Whole." We are worthy of giving and receiving love, we are magnificent in design, we are remarkable, and there is inherent value and meaning in each of our lives. I know this as our authentic truth!

Self-inquiry for your truth will unfold new and remarkable experiences. Honor and trust yourself, your Higher Self. Indeed, commitment to honoring your authentic truth takes courage, patience, loving intention, appreciation, and trust in the process. Challenge yourself to change and to grow… open to your heart's greatest desires. Listen quietly as you open your heart to the possibility of a new perspective. Proceed with kindness and be gentle with yourself. Know that reconnecting with your Authentic Truth is a journey worth making!

HOPE AND POSSIBILITY

I believe that there is good nestling in the heart of all human-
ity, however, good is dismissed, invalidated or suppressed
for fear of the unknown and pain from past experiences. It
is replaced with judgment, condemnation, rejection, denial,
guilt, insecurity, and distrust. These feelings are projected and
re-lived both inwardly and outwardly over and over again...
These same feelings are really an expression of the "self" that
embodies and lives according to the beliefs and perspectives
they have created for themselves; the "self" that longs to be
seen and heard; the "self" that seeks truth. Engaging in hurt-
ful and destructive behaviors is a form of self-sabotage, an
expression of conflict manifesting within. This can present as
being subtle or profound whether directed at others or self.
These behaviors distance us or disengage us from others and
ourselves.

I believe the cause is worth the crusade, and therefore I am
committed. With the principles and practice of courage, faith,
compassion, patience, and perseverance I go forth with my
head held high and my heart wide open offering hope and pos-
sibility. With the "breath" and breadth of gratitude, I make
room in my heart for others. As I learn to embody grace, I am
able to reach deeply into my heart's capacity for mercy to see
what is not so clearly visible, to hear and decipher through

the language of pain and fear, to touch where one knows and feels safe to trust, to smell the desire for love and human connection, and to taste the fruitful bearing of one's heart and soul as they are wholeheartedly nourished and lifted to live their highest intended good. It is my intention to ground the fibers and essence of my being through honor and integrity. I respectfully and lovingly hold myself together with love and light, embodying grace and wisdom from God's love and belief in my ability, trusting HIS words and insights offered to me that I may share boldly and passionately, the worthiness, vulnerability, and deservedness of all humanity.

REMEMBER WHO YOU REALLY ARE

I invite you to come back to your truth. ALL of life's experiences have something to teach us—each has a lesson in it; something that drives us deeper inward, something that will grow us beyond what we presently are aware of.

It is time to identify what is holding you back. What are your thoughts, perspectives, and beliefs? Are there emotional triggers that upset you, remind you of something unpleasant, overwhelm you, or frighten you? Do you have a sense of unease or restlessness in your body, any areas of tension or pain that recurs?

Your outlook on life, the thoughts you have, and the things you are doing or not doing, as well as the beliefs you have about yourself, another person, a situation, or an opportunity, ALL create your reality because you make it so... Your perception of your reality becomes your reality. Your feelings and expectations tie into the creation of your reality. The particular feeling or emotion you associate with an experience is captured as "memory." Simple pleasures can change to painful memories if we link an unpleasant emotion or feeling to them. Do you ever feel that you could be doing better, doing things differently, and living life according to your heart's true desire? Sometimes we just need to be reminded of how special we are.

We easily forget how special we are because we have been hurt or let down in some way. It is easy to lose touch with just how amazing we truly are, how magnificent and capable we are, especially when life's dramas and traumas hit us hard. We lose our way, get off track, often succumbing to a level of personal hardship and despair; self-sabotaging and suffering in the name of love. Much of life's most painful experiences are around the experiences of love that have betrayed or violated us in some way. We lose trust, trust in others and trust in ourselves. We may fear a recurrence of anything that resembles a prior painful experience, and often knowingly or unknowingly disconnect from our deeper core self in order to keep going.

Again, I invite you to come back to your truth so that you may grow and go above and beyond your current capacity and reality.

As I continue to journey
'INTO' my 'SELF', I am
better able to recognize that
there are no mistakes.
Our life experiences teach us,
grow us, move us,
challenge us, prepare us...

~

Every day we have the
opportunity to INSPIRE
HOPE, PEACE, and
POSSIBILITY in
each other's lives!

REFERENCES

1. Zak PJ, Kurzban R, Matzner WT. The neurobiology of trust. *Ann N Y Acad Sci.* 2004;1032:224-227.

2. Zak PJ, Kurzban R, Matzner WT. Oxytocin is associated with human trustworthiness. *Horm Behav.* 2005;48(5):522-527.

3. Zak PJ. The neurobiology of trust. *Sci Am.* 2008;298:88-95.

4. Rein G, Atkinson M, McCraty R. The Physiological and Psychological Effects of Compassion and Anger. *J Advance Med.* 1995; 8 (2): 87-105.

5. Hanson R, Mendius R. *Buddha's Brain: the practical neuroscience of happiness, love & wisdom.* Oakland, CA: New Harbinger Publications;2009:155-160.

6. Dalai Lama Web Site: http://www.dalailama.com/messages/compassion. Accessed August 26, 2014.

ABOUT THE AUTHOR

Deborah is a Physical Therapist and Life Coach, and is a Veteran of the United States Navy. For over two decades, she has been helping people on deeply personal and profound levels to deal with pain, impaired mobility, life-altering change and the uncertainties of life. Her studies and expertise continue to expand in the areas of integrative and complementary therapies, mindfulness and heart centered practices, and working with traumatic injuries and life experiences. Her programs offer simple, realistic, and practical concepts, principles, and strategies for 'piecing' your life together. Deborah strives to keep it real as she promotes having a **positive self-image and a life in harmony, peace, and balance.**

SIGNATURE
Programs and Services

<u>MISSION</u>: Inspire You INTO Empowered
Action to Live Life On Purpose!

EMOTIONAL MUSCLE FITNESS®

- The Heartful Practice of RESILIENCE™
- Heart-Focused Leadership: The Resilient Leader
- HEART'S ALCHEMY SELF-Mastery INTENSIVE®

EMOTIONAL MUSCLE FITNESS®
teaches you how to R.O.A.R.

**GO DEEPER... through a 3-Tier EXPERIENTIAL,
INTEGRATIVE, AND EXPANSIVE PROCESS & PRACTICE**

ACCESS Deeper Self-Awareness and Appreciation — **ALIGN** and **PRACTICE** from your Heart and Soul Centered Power and Truth — **EXPAND** your Mental and Emotional Capacity, Focus, and Tolerance with greater Agility, Aptitude, Fortitude, and Resilience for Sustainable Peak Performance — **ENGAGE** in Life on a "Whole" New Level — **BE** Inspired and Empowered to Take Consistent Action to Live Life on Purpose!

... A uniquely personal and experiential guide to awakening
and exploring SELF-MASTERY...

Individual and Group Coaching, Consulting, Workshops, Retreats
www.emotionalmusclefitness.com

www.ingramcontent.com/pod-product-compliance
Lightning Source LLC
Chambersburg PA
CBHW070117300326
41934CB00035B/1613